WITHDRAWN

BUILT FOR SPEED

FORMULA ONE

Matthew Pitt

HIGH
interest
books

Children's Press
A Division of Grolier Publishing
New York / London / Hong Kong / Sydney
Danbury, Connecticut

Book Design: MaryJane Wojciechowski and Michael DeLisio
Contributing Editor: Jeri Cipriano

Photo Credits: Cover © Indexstock; pp. 4, 12, 24, 30, 33, 35, 36, 41 © AP/World
Wide Photos; pp. 6, 8 © Hulton-Deutsch Collection/Corbis; p. 11 © Dave Houser/
Corbis; p. 15 © George Lepp/Corbis; pp. 16, 20, 26, 38 © AFP/Corbis; pp. 19, 28
© Reuters NewMedia Inc./Corbis; p. 22 © Jerome Prevost; TempSport/Corbis

Visit Children's Press on the Internet at:
http://publishing.grolier.com

Library of Congress Cataloging-in-Publication Data

Pitt, Matthew.
   Formula One / by Matthew Pitt.
      p. cm. — (Built for speed)
   Includes bibliographical references and index.
   ISBN 0-516-23160-X (lib. bdg.) — ISBN 0-516-23263-0 (pbk.)
      1. Automobile racing—Juvenile literature. 2. Grand Prix racing. 3.
   Formula One automobiles. I. Title. II. Built for speed

GV1029.13 .P58 2000
796.72—dc21
                                                        00-063840

CONTENTS

INTRODUCTION

The driver quickly glances up from the track. A race official is waving a colored flag. As the driver zooms by, he sees a blur of bright yellow flag. Another racer has spun off the track. How many others are left in the race? Twelve? Eleven? No time to count. Here comes a sharp corner. Watch out! The driver makes a split-second decision. Hit the brake. Ease up. Steer left—but not too sharply! Made it. That was close!

Formula One cars are among the fastest and most powerful on the planet, and the world of Formula One racing is tense and sometimes scary. The cars are always fast-moving. They move so fast that one hundredth of a second can put you in first place! This book takes you inside this world—with its big races, brave drivers, and swift pit crews. Of course, you'll read about the amazing machines themselves. So buckle up and put both hands on the wheel. Start your engines!

Formula One cars are among the fastest cars on the planet.

Start of Something SPECIAL

Turn back the clock. One hundred years ago, driving a car was a new way to travel. People were just beginning to learn what cars could do. Some people spent a lot of money to make their cars go fast. They wanted to prove to the public that their cars were faster than all others. Auto racing had begun.

The idea of racing for money or trophies is not new. Humans have raced one another on horseback, in sailboats, or at track meets for thousands of years. Why is racing such a popular form of entertainment? It gives people a chance to show off their talents.

As cars improved, the best drivers challenged one another to competitions. They wanted to settle once and for all which automobile was fastest.

This is a racecar from the Grand Prix auto race in 1912.

Racing used to take place in the middle of cities like this. The tires were thin and had spokes like the cars from this race in London.

Races were held anywhere an audience could be found, even at county fairs. There were few rules, and those that did exist often were broken. Some drivers even cheated during competitions. Early races could be unsafe. The audience had little protection from the cars. Being too near a speeding car could lead to serious injuries! Still, people came from miles around to watch racing events.

RACING AROUND THE WORLD AND THROUGH THE CITY

The United States wasn't the only country caught up in racing fever. Europeans also were discovering the thrill. Racing cars were much different then. Their tires were thinner and had spokes, like the wheels of a bicycle. Engines were heavier and were put in the front of cars. Races were different, too. In 1895, there were no racetracks. Races were held right in the middle of cities! To be a spectator, all you had to do was look out your window!

The first race occurred on the streets of France. The event was called the Grand Prix, which means "grand prize" in French. Grand Prix racing is another name for Formula One racing. In that first Grand Prix race, the winner's car drove about 70 mph (112.7 km/h). Today's cars can reach speeds more than three times that speed!

Thanks to the Grand Prix, racing became more popular than ever. People wanted to know which country could produce the fastest car and the best driver. They wanted to crown a world champion. But the safety and rules of motor racing were shaky. In 1950, a group called the Federation International de l'Automobile (FIA) was formed. Its mission was to oversee the sport of racing. Under FIA leadership, a World Championship began in 1950.

The FIA ruled on how long cars could be, how much they could weigh, and which engines could be used. They also worked to make races safer for both drivers and spectators. Faster cars were designed. Tires were built to grip the road better. The FIA still governs motor racing today and continues to make the sport stronger.

The Grand Prix made racing popular with large groups of people like this crowd at the Grand Prix in Vancouver, Canada.

Catch Them
IF YOU CAN

Formula One cars have made great progress. Today's models can go from 0 to 100 mph (161 km/h) in less than 5 seconds. What's their top speed? On circuits with the longest straight-aways—stretches of track without curves—they have reached 230 mph (370 km/h). If we ran that fast, we could get from one end of a football field to the other in 2 seconds!

Many improvements have been made to reach these record-breaking speeds. Racing tracks, or circuits, are safer. Drivers are better trained. Pit crews are faster and smarter. They study the racetracks. They test each piece of equipment carefully. They spend long nights preparing for races. We'll consider all of these things later. For now, let's focus on the cars.

Formula One racetracks are safer today, like this one which held the Monaco Grand Prix (1998).

THE SPEED OF LIGHT

As races became more popular, Formula One designers realized something. The less cars weighed, the faster they could go. Imagine having to move around with a stack of books on your back. The extra weight of the books would create a resistance, or drag. In racing, drag slows cars down and weakens their performance.

It became important to build lighter and lighter cars. The chassis, or frame, of an old Formula One car was made from heavy sheet metal. Over time, the heavy metals were replaced with lighter materials, such as aluminum. The engine

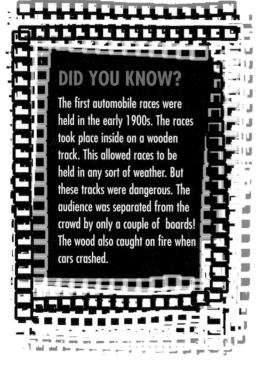

DID YOU KNOW?

The first automobile races were held in the early 1900s. The races took place inside on a wooden track. This allowed races to be held in any sort of weather. But these tracks were dangerous. The audience was separated from the crowd by only a couple of boards! The wood also caught on fire when cars crashed.

Old Formula One cars used to be shaped like cigars.

was moved from the front to the rear of the car. This change eliminated the need for a long drive shaft. A drive shaft helps get the engine's power to the rear tires. But with the new design, the engine was already right beside the rear tires.

Formula One cars also got faster by being built lower to the ground. Older cars were shaped like cigars. But new technology made

Formula One drivers sit low to the ground.

the cars flatter. Today, they are so low to the ground that the drivers don't even sit up to drive. Instead, they drive in a kind of reclining position, somewhere between sitting and lying down.

Just as the chassis was made out of a lighter material, so were the new engines. Today's engines also have a lot more power. They are twice as large as regular engines, and have more cylinders. Cylinders are the chambers through which the fuel passes. The more cylinders an engine has, the more fuel there is to power the car. Regular cars have four, six, or eight cylinders. But a Formula One engine has ten or twelve!

GET A GRIP!

Formula One cars soon became too light. They began losing their grip on the track. Vehicles kept spinning off the circuit. Speeds were faster than ever. But drivers were in too much danger.

Designers turned to gravity for help. The minimum weight of a Formula One car was raised to 1,309 pounds (589 kg). That's still very light. Regular cars weigh twice as much. Designers spent a lot of time improving tires. Having excellent tires is important for cars to get a good grip on the track. Formula One drivers get eleven sets of tires for each race. These tires are a little taller and twice as wide as regular car tires. Four sets of tires are "wet" tires.

They are used only when it rains. These wet tires contain grooves which help push away rain during a race so the tires won't slip.The tires that are used in dry weather are called slicks. They are completely bald! They look like their treads have completely worn off. Because the tires are flat, more of the tire rubber can touch the track at all times. This helps the tires gain the maximum grip, or traction, on the circuit. Grip is very important for both speed and safety. Before every race, Formula One tires are wrapped in a heated blanket. This helps improve the tires' traction during the race.

CARS WITH WINGS?

Aerodynamics measures how air affects an object's movement. If a car is not aerodynamic, wind cannot flow smoothly over it. Instead, the wind creates drag, which slows down the car. Designers discovered how important downforce was to a Formula One's speed. To produce more downforce, they put wings on the cars. Of course, these are special wings. They are not like airplane wings. Instead of lifting a Formula One off the ground, these wings help it stay on the ground. There are two wings on a Formula One. One is in the back. The other is near the nose. Both can be adjusted to produce extra downforce. If there

Formula One cars have wings in the front and the back.

is not enough downforce, the air will push up a Formula One. Then the tires are less able to grip the track. This means it is easier for the driver to lose control of the car. But if the wrong amount of downforce is produced, the car may not steer well.

As you can see, a Formula One racecar has advertisements clearly showing.

THIS CAR IS
BROUGHT TO YOU BY...

Designers spend millions of dollars improving Formula One cars. From where does the money come? Advertising. In the 1970s, the costs of building quality cars skyrocketed. Racing teams offered to advertise for companies in exchange for money. Department stores, oil companies, and clothing makers all wanted in on the action! That's why Formula One cars look like billboards. They're covered with the logos of major companies that paid for, or sponsored, them. The drivers even wear logos on their uniforms.

Safe and Snug in the COCKPIT

Grand Prix cars must be light, low, and compact. So Formula One drivers have to put up with a snug fit. In fact, the seat, or cockpit, of each car is specially molded to fit the shape of its driver! There is only enough room for a person to move arms and feet. A Grand Prix race lasts 90 minutes. That's a long time to sit still. Drivers wear special seat belts which lock at six different points. In a crash, a driver pushes a button in the center. This releases the driver from the harness. The steering wheel is also removable, in case the driver has to make a quick exit.

What if the car catches fire? Formula One drivers wear four layers of fire-resistant clothes, including socks, gloves, and long

Formula One drivers wear special seat bealts and have a snug fit inside their cars.

underwear. These clothes keep drivers safe in blazes up to 1,300° F (704.4° C). In addition, drivers wear protective helmets. The helmets are very strong. A stone traveling at 300 mph (483 km/h) could hit them and not even crack their exterior.

THE INFORMATION HIGHWAY

There are a lot of gadgets in the tiny cockpit space. They all help the Formula One go at top speed. Two levers let drivers switch gears with simple flicks of the wrist. Buttons warn the driver of problems with oil pressure or engine overheating. Drivers speak with their pit crews through radio contact. Drivers can read their cars' speed. They even can see how long it took to drive a lap. Some cockpit buttons are top secret!

Formula One drivers wear protective clothing that keeps them safe in case of a fire.

They help teams keep their competitive edge. All these buttons and displays help drivers. They give drivers information and let them concentrate on sharp turns and high speeds. It's like having an invisible copilot in the cockpit. Grand Prix racing has driven into the computer age!

PREPARE TO QUALIFY

The days leading up to Sunday's race are almost as tense as the race itself. On Friday and Saturday, drivers practice up to sixty laps on the circuit. They spend only 1 hour each day driving. Their other hours are filled with meetings. The teams discuss strategies and possible technical problems with their cars. These meetings are the last chance to work out problems. Racers test their steering on sharp turns. If necessary, teams make adjustments. Wings may need fixing to produce more downforce. Tires may need adjustments. On practice days, the racetrack becomes a laboratory.

Saturday afternoon is the time to qualify. Drivers get twelve laps to prove they're fast enough to compete. Qualifying is all about speed. Drivers fuel up just enough to last twelve laps. That way, they won't have even an ounce of extra weight dragging them down. All the cars reach incredible speeds, but only the best drivers qualify. The driver who records the fastest lap time is awarded the "pole position." This car gets a slight head start in the race, and will have the best approach to the first corner. Because split seconds count in Formula One races, everyone wants that pole position.

Finally, it's inspection time. Trained FIA officials inspect each Formula One car. The officials are called scrutineers. Scrutineers have a checklist

During qualifying, drivers compete for the "pole position."

Sarah Fisher is one of the women who qualified to race in the Indianapolis 500.

with forty-four items on it. They check to see if anything is missing, loose, or poorly constructed. A car can be disqualified if just one item is not perfect. Teams that make it through inspection need time to rest. The race will start in just a few hours.

WOMEN TRAILBLAZERS

In 1909, Alice Ramsey made the shocking announcement that she would drive from New York City to Los Angeles. Big deal? At that time, it was. Men thought women couldn't handle driving cars. But Ramsey made the journey safely. Today, women drive everywhere. And in the year 2000, two women qualified to race in the Indianapolis 500 for the first time.

FORMULA ONE FLOPS

New Formula One cars have come out over the years. But not every one is an improvement. One team built a Formula One with six wheels. The two wheels in the back were normal. But the front four wheels were very small. The team hoped that this would improve the car's grip and aerodynamics. But the tires wore down too quickly. One of the first drivers to use wings put them on stilts in the back of the car. During the race, one wing collapsed from the speed and the wind. Still, it always pays to

Get Ready...
GET SET...

Engines are revving. Tires are turning from side to side. A Grand Prix race is underway. But wait. The cars aren't going that fast. Is there a problem?

Not at all. Just before the official start, race-cars go through a final practice. Formula One teams push their cars into position at the front of the track. This area is called the starting grid. The cars line up in order of how they qualified. The pole position car is in front. The next-fastest car is second, and so on. Drivers circle the track one last time to warm up. This is called a formation lap. Competitors weave their vehicles left and right. They are warming the tires to get better traction. They're also testing the tire pressure and how their cars are

Drivers go through one last formation lap before the start of the race.

handling. The cars drive the formation lap at about 110 mph (177 km/h). That's a high speed for a regular car. But that speed is nothing for a Formula One.

At last, the drivers see the green flag waving wildly. The race has begun!

MOVIN' ON UP

Just staying on the racetrack is hard enough. But Formula One drivers have to put in more effort if they want to either take the lead or maintain it. The best drivers are not just fast. They're smart!

There are strategies drivers use to overtake other vehicles. One of the more famous techniques is called slipstreaming. This is when a driver sneaks up behind the car directly ahead of him. The lead car has to battle high winds. The car behind the lead car is less affected by these winds and has better aerodynamics. Just at the right moment on a straightaway, the

Formula One drivers use a technique called slipstreaming to get ahead.

second car slips to the side of the lead car and pulls ahead. Meanwhile, the lead car continues to battle the wind, and it falls behind.

PIT STOP

One of the most exciting times in a Grand Prix race occurs when the cars aren't moving. These are pit stops. Now the focus switches from the speed of the cars to the speed of the mechanics.

During a pit stop, cars exit the circuit and come to a screeching halt. Eighteen mechanics immediately jump into position. In the pit, having fast hands is very important. Crew members are all aware of where to go and what to do. That's because they are in constant radio communication with the driver. They already know if the Formula One car is having problems. Once the car rolls in, it's up to the pit crew to fix the problems — in a matter of seconds! To do this takes constant practice. Crew members learn to break down big tasks into smaller ones. During pit stops, they change tires, refuel cars, and give drivers drinks—all in 10 seconds! The pit crew puts three members on each tire. Two people replace the old tire with a new one. The third mechanic fastens the new tire with an air wrench.

Two other crew members operate the large refueling hose. There's also a chief mechanic,

A pit crew repairs a Formula One racecar in a matter of seconds!

an assistant refueler, and an engine technician. It can get crowded and tense in the pit. But safety comes first. If pit crew members aren't careful, they could burn themselves on the car's hot chassis. Or if fuel spills on the track, it could start a fire.

Pit stops are vital to a team's success. At a recent race in Spain, the crew of a pole position driver had trouble refueling. The pit stop took 18 seconds. The driver fell from first to fifth place. Meanwhile, another driver's pit stop took less than 7 seconds. Because of this, he went from runner-up to winner!

EARLY RETIREMENT

Fewer than half of the Formula One vehicles in each race cross the finish line. Some cars collide during tight turns. Some spin off the track. Others have electrical problems or tires that get punctured by loose objects. When an accident occurs, a vehicle that looks like a police car enters the track. This is the pace car. When drivers see the pace car, they must slow down. They drive behind it until race officials are sure the damaged Formula One has been cleared from the track.

A crashed Formula One car has crews to clean up the damage.

VICTORY!

Using one last blast of speed, one car crosses the finish line first. The checkered flag whips around in all directions. Winning at Formula One takes a delicate mix of skill, determination,

and luck. A point system is awarded to drivers. Ten points go to the winner, six points for second place, four for third, three for fourth, two for fifth, and one for sixth. After a full year of competing, the driver with the most points is named world champion.

A driver who finishes sixth is happy to accept his one point. He hopes he can finish stronger next time. Meanwhile, the first-place winner can't celebrate for long. He will have to work even harder next time. And the next race is never far off. It may be only a week away.

Racing is very exciting. It can be heart-stopping to watch on TV. It's

When the race is over, an official waves a checkered flag.

even more fun to watch live at a stadium. There are many great circuits in the United States. The Indianapolis Motor Speedway is the most famous. But there are also great circuits in Michigan, Arizona, and Pennsylvania.

People have a great time watching the races at a stadium, like these people at the Indianapolis Motor Speedway.

DRIVER'S ED

Would you like to be a Formula One driver? Many of today's superstars got their start in school. There are many racing schools in the world. Students begin by driving sedans. They take instruction from professional racecar drivers who sit beside them. They learn when to brake, how to stay in the racing line through sharp corners, and how to recognize mechanical problems. Students work their way up to racing single-seaters, which are similar to Formula One cars. Some schools even send their top students to all-expenses-paid races. The old saying is true: Experience is the best teacher!

NEW WORDS

aerodynamics how wind and air propel or slow
   down a moving object
chassis the frame of a Formula One
   racing vehicle
circuit another name for track
cockpit the space where a driver of a Formula
   One car sits
competition an event or test of skill between
   two or more people
downforce a force of air that pushes the tires of
   a Formula One car down to the racetrack
govern to make laws or rules for a
   group of people
pit stops the times when racecar drivers stop for
   car repairs and refueling
scrutineers officials who inspect Formula One
   cars before a race

NEW WORDS

spectators people who watch sporting events for enjoyment

sponsor one who helps pay for the costs of making a Formula One car

straightaways long stretches of racetrack without any curves

traction the amount of grip Formula One tires have on the track

For Further READING

Benson, Michael. *Dale Earnhardt*. Broomall, PA: Chelsea House Publishers, 1996.

Huff, Richard M. *Formula One Racing*. Broomall, PA: Chelsea House Publishers, 1997.

Kirkwood, Jon. *The Fantastic Book of Car Racing*. Brookfield, CT: Millbrook Press, 1997.

McKenna, A.T. *Formula 1 Racing*. Minneapolis, MN: ABDO Publishing Company, 1998.

Olney, Ross Robert. *Lyn St. James: Driven to Be First*. Minneapolis, MN: The Lerner Publishing Group, 1997.

RESOURCES

Web Sites

American Racing 'Zine—Racing On The Web!
www.racecar.com
This site presents up-to-date information about competitions—including race results, qualifying results, and point standings. You can check the NASCAR schedule to see if there's a race in your area.

Professional Sports Car Racing
www.professionalsportscar.com
This is the official Web site of Professional Sports Car Racing. It contains current news, schedules, and race results.

RESOURCES

U.S. Grand Prix Web Site

www.usgpindy.com

This is the official Web site of the U. S. Grand Prix at Indianapolis. The site gives the history of Formula One racing. It also includes photos, news, and movies to download.

INDEX

INDEX

About the Author

Matthew Pitt is a freelance writer living in Brooklyn, New York. He has written magazine articles, short stories, and books while living in cities such as Austin, Texas, Washington D.C., and Los Angeles, California.